MW01289339

Consistently East

By Matthew Eiford-Schroeder

Edited by Christopher Luna

Printed Matter Vancouver
Vancouver, WA
2018

Consistently East
By Matthew Eiford-Schroeder

Edited by Christopher Luna
For Printed Matter Vancouver

Book Design by Christopher Luna and
Toni Lumbrazo Luna

Christopher Luna thanks Soma Feldmar for
her assistance.

Map by Calvin Braly

Published by Printed Matter Vancouver
Vancouver, Washington
USA
www.printedmattervancouver.com
printedmattervancouver@gmail.com

ISBN-13: 978-1721862375
ISBN-10: 1721862374

Copyright 2018
By Matthew Eiford-Schroeder
All Rights Reserved

TABLE OF CONTENTS

Map by Calvin Braly.....7
Consistently East.....8
Hand on Pencil, Scrape the Page.....10
A Nephew of the Last Cowboys.....11
Patrick.....12
Preparation.....13
Leaving Day.....15
London.....16
Budapest Again.....17
A Woman is Beaten in Belgrade.....18
Greece.....20
Istanbul.....21
      Search for a Dot within a Sprawl.....21
      The Call to Prayer.....21
      Continue the Search for a Dot within a Sprawl.....22
      Have Things to See.....22
      The Call to Prayer.....22
      On a Bus Station Sandwich Board.....23
      Ramadan.....23
      Under a White Scarf.....24
      Just Dark Eyes.....24
      She Has Come to See the Same Thing as Me.....24
      Exchange Rate.....25
The Attitude of T-Shirts for Sale in Every Beach Town.....26
Sunny Beach, Bulgaria: Birthplace of Intimidancing.....27
Lunch on the Move.....29
Ukraine.....30
The Unwieldy Bear.....32
Temporarily Without Proof.....33
Hearts and Minds.....34
2 AM Kazakhstan.....35
Who Did You Meet My Green Eyed Son?..... 38
Driving.....39
A 1.2 liter Engine.....40
The Formation of Dingus Kahnvoy.....41
Supplement to Navigation.....42
The Steppe.....43
Night Pooping on the Outskirts of the Gobi Desert.....52
Too Hot to Roll the Windows Down.....53

A Nomad Smile.....55
Knowing Where to Look.....56
Arrival.....58
Test of Skill.....59
MONGOLIAN STRIP CLUB.....60
You Can Always Depend on the Kindness of Strangers.....64
The Smile that Turned North to South.....65
Let Go.....66
Negotiating a Guide.....67
A Lovely Day in Tsagaasaanur in Three Parts.....68
The Death of Wilderness.....71
Shaman Vomit.....73
Bad Sex on a Stomach Bug.....75
The End of a Tender Tap.....76
Korea.....78
San Francisco Layover.....79
Handicap Access, National Parks, and the Highway System:
The Three Great Beacons of the American Attempt.....80
The Dream of Dakota.....82
Heritage Marker.....83
A Familiar Face.....84
Boom, Bust and Goodbye.....85
When the Trickle Down Lands.....87
Being Driven.....89
She is Happy.....90
Return to Ritual.....91
Return to Ritual 2.....92
A Nice Lie, If Only for an Evening.....93
The Night I Became a Memory of Myself.....94
Brain Injury.....95

About the Author.....97
About Printed Matter Vancouver.....98

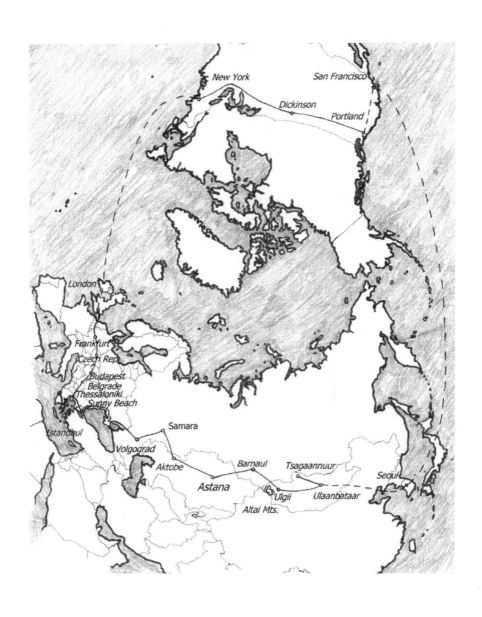

Map by Calvin Braly

Consistently East

What is adventure in the time of Google Maps? If hardship is what separates an adventure from a vacation, how does one reconcile the ease of travel with the challenges one faces? What does that mean for men who were boys dreaming of adventure? Being a white, straight, English-speaking male in the time of the Internet and the airplane, I have more access to any point on the globe than the vast majority of humans who have ever lived. With enough effort, I can move any place out of imagination and into reality. Access began to build an understanding of what was done to the world to create this ease of movement; what the world did in response. What I do to the world as I move through it, and what the world does to me. Connection means it is impossible to move without pushing or pulling on someone, somewhere.

In 2012 I flew across the Atlantic Ocean from New York with my friend Patrick, and we drove from London to Mongolia in a charity rally. When he left, I fell in a quick petit love and followed her on her quest to see a shaman. I then flew to Seoul. From there I returned to my family on the West Coast of the United States. Wanting a soft return to New York, I drove with Cody and Amy to North Dakota to work in the oil fields before finally arriving back in Brooklyn (my starting point) by train. A lot of damage and beauty has transpired in the world and myself since we went around each other.

For me oblivion floated on fists. When I arrived back in New York I worked as a bouncer to pay for my next adventure, until one night when I was punched in the head around 30 times while on the job. I watched the places I had traveled to change while recovering from a brain injury. In my fog I would watch the news and see what was happening to the places that had shaped the way I see humanity, the places I loved as I was trying to rebuild my self. The news became more tangible. A clear line of movement in my memory connected me to these places. They were not part of a separate world barricaded from me. I knew in a way beyond intellect that imagination wasn't the only way to see the peoples affected by headlines.

I saw protests change Ukraine's government. The peaceful drive I made into Russia is no longer possible. I saw that bombs had gone off in Istanbul near the site of one of the most spiritual experiences of my life. Later, the last free newspaper was taken over by the government. Then there was a failed coup. I watched refugees flee the Syrian civil war as they tried to head North on the same route that had let me drive south the year before. That same war sent gas prices down and dried the money flow that brought me to North Dakota. Those same falling oil prices and U.S. sanctions on the land I drove over in Ukraine took the value out of the Ruble I used to buy beer. Threats against South Korea made me think of faces rather than numbers.

Traveling by land for over 10,000 miles, the people and history bleed into each other. Villains become heroes and vice versa with enough distance from those they killed and those who benefited. In constant love, rage, and greed, we unite and divide on a very tactile and traversable land. Compartmentalization becomes catastrophically inaccurate. Contradiction becomes inevitable. These times and places are where I hid when I was trapped in an imploding self. They were what I could connect to.

I needed to remember the time in my life when I had the most agency in order to crawl out of the time when I had the least. To connect who I would become on the other side of recovery with who I was before I was made aware of a different kind of destruction. I wrote these poems when the world stopped shaking enough for me to collect and organize words again. I had to rebuild myself, take an inventory of memories, then create. To begin to live in a world that had changed in a self that was no longer the same, but both not completely severed from the trauma and beauty of the past.

It would be a mistake for the reader to believe anyone mentioned in this book views the world or this time the same way I do. The slight distance required to stand next to me is more than enough to lead to a different view. Also, they have been hit in the head significantly less.

Matthew Eiford-Schroeder

Hand on Pencil, Scrape the Page

Beaten to the edge of destruction
nothing to push against

I cannot stand for very long anymore
I sit and write, backwards
into the un-wired rubble of myself
seek the words of the memories I have left

stack them into something I can use
try to stumble out of scattered oblivion

A Nephew of the Last Cowboys

I was a baby bombarded
by the madness of a failed war.
Whiskey recalled the screams of a rice field
that followed me as I rolled over and
      crawled.

I was a boy saved by my Mom
taken to my grandparents' cattle farm.
I was loved as we coaxed beef from land
rugged labor a respite from my rage.

My dreams grew in the American West.
I crave the wild.

I was a man in New York
when the farm was turned into modern living solutions
fighting drunks for the safety of dancing girls
to pay for my tangents: art, love, whiskey,
                  wilderness in Alaska,
                  adventure in Europe.

Never satisfied with my catch
I stared at maps
and found Mongolia.

The world wants to
show me something,
and I am going to look.

Patrick

Riding under a pompadour
& a 20-dollar Texas arm tattoo
art school redneck
subscribes to *The Economist*
and too many shots of Goldschläger.
Snake eyes and the hard good bye.

He does not understand that pain hurts
and will sculpt an owl with tits.

We became brothers debating cowboy boots.

He helped me mourn the death of a lion with a bottle of
Razzmatazz.

He has the heart of 10-year-old boy
who loves his dog, his Mom and his dad, and his country.
Disruptive Boy Scout.

He does not understand what we are about to do.
It will not stop him from doing it.
He knows he would regret not doing it
so he will risk love and money.

He is done wearing sleeves for the summer.

TEXAS

Together we form HURRICANE MATTRICK!!!!
Together we drag race our sanity.
Women love us almost as much as we hate ourselves.

Preparation

Patrick has heard about a drive to Mongolia
from some Dutch customers

We decide to do it: rum shots
                       a man and his maps
Iran is a limiting factor in which way around the Black Sea
30 day double entry
                   which countries require a Carnet de Passages?
water purifiers   Nagorno-Karabakh
ATM?
        list of exchange rates

buying a car in England over the internet
insurance can be bought at the Turkish border
        travel insurance   tents

Is the Georgia-Russia border open?
Maybe we can meet up tonight.
This is a safe thing to do?

the state department warns U.S. citizens traveling to
Do we need shots?   EMT classes 12 hours a week and 3 jobs
Visa Expediters for Russia and Kazakhstan
Turkmenistan visa process is very complicated
do not overstay a Russian visa

bandits   ferry from Baku
        how do you say sorry in all of these languages
torn rotator cuff after I got hit by a car   backpacks

I really am going to miss her

3 deserts 2 mountain ranges
                   Do we need vaccinations?   Camera
                   fundraiser for the orphanage   Car Jack

list of closest embassies' phone numbers and addresses
in all 19 countries
Patrick is not taking this seriously.   How cold does it get?
always have a shovel in your Oh Shit Kit

Holy Shit the Gobi desert.
Motorists should avoid
confrontations with aggressive drivers in Bulgaria. Drivers are
known to speed, swerve into oncoming traffic, go the wrong way
on divided highways, and participate in other dangerous
activities.

Motorists should exercise caution and avoid altercations with
the drivers of such vehicles, which may be driven by armed
organized crime figures.

What is a fake country? Transitria
if we go to jail there there is no embassy

Ferry in the Black Sea?   10,000 miles
but most importantly
a tourist bends the world to meet him
a traveler bends to meet the world

Leaving Day

In red she looked as if she jumped out of a trumpet
        in Langston Hughes's Harlem.
Memories of NYU and Martha's Vineyard floated in a statue of a
woman dispensing nachos and Bud Light.
Was art worth being a waitress?
She has too much to say to be predicted
Her feet can feel what the lashes have done to
        the shoulders she stands on.
I want to flood her body, to break her brain one last time
        hold her in a moment of enjoyed confusion.
How can I leave a house with so many rooms?
Over a cup of coffee we ran out of time.

My old friend has to drop off a survival kit:
        metal epoxy, Iodine tablets, bandages,
        US 20s and singles, heat blankets.
"You don't have to do anything smart you just can't do anything
stupid" he says as he means "I love you."
Over knives and maps we ran out of time.

She turned off her phone to better connect with her desserts,
        when she showed up.
Her absence was always preceded by a text.
The warmth was worth the fluidity.
She liked to swim with the wildlife too much
        for the comfort of Parma.
She wanted to flood my body, to break my brain one last time
        hold me in a moment of enjoyed calm.
Over fried rice we ran out of time.

With a full backpack I stand on the streets of New York
I who always thought she could stack humanity a little bit higher
        to keep them both from collapsing.
Over rum we ran out of time.

I have forced the life I have always wanted upon myself.

London

We have left America
Without leaving our logos behind
Different accents sling the same slogans
We are the taste of a new generation.

On Carnabie or Canal
Debate whose version of *The Office*
Better encapsulated working in an office.

There will be no maturity on the train to Cocksfair.
Dangerous neighborhoods are quaint without handguns.

We sleep on the floor of a friend who will light Bob Costas
Who will announce the feats that represent
How far the human body can go
Brought to you by the logos we never left.

We stock up on what we may need
Because you can find it here.

Budapest Again

I reminisce with my river
I used to work in this hostel, this island
back then my naiveté stopped me
conned on the street
I made these beds to make my way home
nothing but time and cheap wine to celebrate the moronic
beauty of youth
watched the light linger in the ripples
and make new lovers out of all possible passports

three years later on this same patio
the post-Soviet crumble has been painted over with WiFi
the light no longer shared
a new light selected by each individual
nothing has been lost, only ignored
the ripples still make their way to the Black Sea
un-witnessed   un-remembered un-loved

fully stocked with a lesser naiveté for tomorrow
I will chase the call I never stopped hearing

                              "further east"

A Woman is Beaten in Belgrade

a scream takes my sleep in the morning
    a woman
across a courtyard behind a window and a wall
    two men
try their hardest to mend the broken parts of themselves by breaking
the complexity of another

a beating.

I don't know a number to call
what I do to the door might be considered worse than what
    they do behind it
in a place I understood I could take this choice from these men

she will be here tomorrow
    I will not
if I take this from them what will they take from her when I'm gone?
when I'm down the road drinking beer feeling heroic
and she is being blamed for what they did and what I did about it
whose life would I have made better?

my obligation is as a witness
every fist into her form
the men watch me watching them
and continue without shame
bruises as the blood she owns
rushes to pool in the skin she owns

each blow a trespasser, thief and dictator
    I watch
as one of the men backs up for a running start
the other kneels and yells at her in a place to deflect the kick
they are not going to kill her
so I remain a witness

they turn the world to walls with force
choice cannot survive the free fall of violence
small men infect their minutia into the multitudes
    contained in another

her body can give life but it can't give mine
the kind with car keys

when they have stuffed the caverns inside themselves
    with enough of her
    to dull the echo they can't stand to hear

in this easily broken quiet she shakes and sobs
until it is time to stand in a smaller world
without ground or floors

Greece

When the money is stagnant
the water still moves to the sea
rubs the buildings the way the wind rubs the rocks
trickles down and turns potholes into puddles
        for stray dogs to lick.

The men are too loud for deceptive business practices.
Every transaction involves yelling until we accept free tomatoes.
We get thrown out of an ice cream store
for trying to pay for our ice cream during backgammon.

The tires are cheap and the coffee is free.
The network of friends and cousins is FDIC insured
        and iron clad.
The banks close before 3.
Afternoons are too hot for capitalism
        so we eat squid by the sea.

Women proudly rub their bellies—
they know where the mechanism that
makes life greater than the sum of its parts is.
To keep this kingdom of the past
life must flow unabsorbed by the nonsense of now.

From a hemisphere away
cast in pixels
my niece giggles for the first time.
Is all I'm doing seeing how the rest of the world
        is living a life I don't think I want?

Istanbul

we wake up to peel away the West
the faces of the men with guns who check documents
      no longer look like mine
for the first time my words can reduce my world to the distance
      contained within a tape measure
I am until today a stranger to the illegal idea
as sure as I am that Ataturk is the greatest, I am unaware of an
      Armenian genocide
what kind of hate can be found where suffering cannot be
      expressed recklessly?
with stamps and insurance us eagles are legal to begin the

Search for a Dot within a Sprawl

in Istanbul traffic
aggression is order
patience is punished
what works in the Midwest will not work in the Mideast
rage is right of way
take all distance immediately
cognitive dissonance is hell on a clutch
princess* flirts with a coma as we pull off the shoulder
      of an on ramp
for the first time it is heard

The Call to Prayer

a sound floods the sky with mystery and energy
a sound from action movies, establishing the danger
the sculpted torso of a reluctant hero with perfect hair and
cheekbones is in
      a sound from CNN, establishing the danger the sculpted
      torso of a reluctant hero with perfect hair and cheekbones
      is in

* "Princess" was a GPS system that worked poorly.

a sound to open-ended substitute the Cold War
a sound that satisfies the little boy who always wanted to be
    somewhere else
as suddenly as it started it stops, and we

Continue the Search for a Dot within a Sprawl

truckers use phones to find English to find the Hilton for us
we're given a list of exits as princess wakes up
we race her battery to find our friend
Patrick finds a way to remember how to drive a race car,
    and turn us into water in a river of boulders
we can move the way they move,
    in competition instead of politeness
next to the national beer of Turkey we find Shimmin and we

Have Things to See

the Bosporus draws blood and beauty pools in the stretch marks
    left by a long game of tug o' war
the Hagia Sophia bears the bruises of her jealous lovers'
temporary grasps
we haggle for trinkets made in China
some things never change
as it is heard again

The Call to Prayer

A sound floods the sky with mystery and energy
my ears drink in the centuries
a blanket folded again and again and again and again and again
and again and again
    and again
grows thicker every year

repetition penetrates the pull of time
carves a space for the soul to hide, from the endless march of
action movement

I begin to take comfort in a blanket that is not my own
      as quickly as it starts it stops
      and I see the forbidden

On a Bus Station Sandwich Board

with what is in my pocket I could buy a ticket to Tehran
land of Rumi and Hafiz—since '79, treason for me

in the time since I was born the places I have just been
      and am going to
Belgrade, Budapest, Bratislava and Volgograd
have stopped being treason for me

because the old men still shout
to listen to the sweet talk of girls and boys is still treason for me

oh, beautiful men and women of Persia, I dream of a day when
Matt is no longer one couplet short, and our touch is no longer
treason for me

Ramadan

after we kill these beers
put on your long pants, bro
let's curse the mosque
on our way in the streets
people from Detroit to Jakarta
are turning themselves into sugar and light
pure
the parts of us that come from paradise pushed to the front
take off your shoes
every sharp thing has been scraped smooth
raw
my foot feels the bow in the marble step
from the repetitive weight of the faithful traveling
      to the geometry of transcendence
in the places I'm allowed

all of me is welcome
but there are spaces just for women

Under a White Scarf

I see the life of a mother's mouth
as she fights with her son
with James Dean on the front of his shirt
he breaks away from her blue jeans
as she calls for him to come back
they dart past

Just Dark Eyes

floating in Negative Space
black cloth creates her omission
thin enough to be pushed by the wind
thick enough to separate the world
her face is too dangerous for the public
or the public is too dangerous for her face
so her life is unseen
only the men close enough to love, nurture, beat, and rape her
      can see if her silent lips shift, or perhaps
I am coward
projecting fantasies of sex suffering salvation and housework
onto her canvas without consulting her
from a place I don't understand

She Has Come to See the Same Thing as Me

faith condensed into a frame
to hang the worlds known and unknown
the beauty of tradition bursting with enough sound, kindness,
and energy to connect the living to the dead and the un-born
all three sit inseparable in a hard-won space
hand in hand
in light and sugar

Exchange Rate

Large amounts of money are worth trading
small amounts we turn into candy
which will hold its value in 400 meters
when motivation changes colors

The Attitude of T-Shirts for Sale in Every Beach Town

"IF YOU AIN'T TITS OR
 A JET SKI GET SHOT IN THE
FACE."- Big Dick Jet Truck

Sunny Beach, Bulgaria
Birthplace of Intimidancing

On a paper placemat we found our sinkhole destiny:
     a Black Sea town with no history,
     except Papa needs small bills.

We will have two rum and cokes, OK I bring four.
Five for one margaritas, shots 10 at a time.
My soul has turned to discount microwave pizza
          under the weight of exceptional drink specials.

These girls are too young and drunk to operate their breasts.
My grandma and the feminist blogosphere
prevent a buxom catastrophe.

Now that you mention it, I would love to shoot a bow and arrow.
Omnipresent techno starts at 5 PM.
My Danish party boy alter ego wants to light the fuse,
But our new friend is in distress.

He has drunk goobers who are too cool to pay their bill.
My rage will not stop my dancing,
my dancing will not stop my helping.

I take a position behind my ally.
I create new vectors.
The goobers' problem grows in complexity
          as the man with an encyclopedia of bar-fights in his eyes
          vigorously tries to trade bodies with Gloria Estefan.

A peace is negotiated.

I tell myself, through my friend,
          that I won't be here tomorrow.
We both know it is a lie.

They have paid off the Fabergé Eggs of Women to dance
    in high heels and bikinis to keep that from happening.
I'm convinced one of them will be the Gloria Steinem of Bulgaria.

Lunch on the Move

We are spacemen from the TV,
but our needs are known upon arrival
the same since childhood.

Synchronized biology substitutes for language.
Mothers see our stupidity and think of their sons.
Compelled to put on a table what their mothers taught them to
take:
      the sun dancing with their dirt.

We convert chemicals and
blind commonality creates concern.

They worry about our next meals:
Romania is a safe country, Moldova is a poor country.
The Turks can strip a car in minutes.
Don't trust the Russians.
Mongolians are savages.

I grow concerned about what else our commonality creates
      when the sun and the soil won't sing.
The needs of a child can always be taken from a neighbor
      unless they take it first.

Ukraine

Delayed by cheap drinks in Bulgaria, and a severed exhaust manifold in Romania, there will be no time for Ukraine.

Wheat   wheat

       wHEat   whEat sunflowers wheat

If a Ukrainian had no time to drive across Nebraska
      as fast as I had to drive across Ukraine
      we would have had the same take away

wheat   wheat

        wheaT   wheat   wheaT
suNflowers

wheat

This town looks like it was doing a lot better a long time ago.

 wheat, wHeat, wheat, sUnflowErs, Wheat

I would gladly give my left testicle to sleep with these women. I would gladly give the other one to never fight any of these men. They both seem nice, but I have no idea what they are saying.

       WhEaT

     wheat   wheat   wheat   wHeAt

sunfloweRs

wHeat

Does that guy need that AK-47, or does he just like it?

wHeat   I'm sorry I missed you

The Unwieldy Bear

We have underestimated the vastness of wheat, wreckage,
    and rust.
Roads are not labeled, maps aren't oriented north.
Goods and people do not travel easy on a ruptured ribbon
    of asphalt, left to drown and dry in the Volga River Valley.

Buildings have hangovers.
The inhabitants will not be sober enough to consider one.
Our presence is an insult.
Grocery stores have the precarious calm
    of an after hours strip club in South Carolina.
On the street we're never more than an excuse away
    from a fist fight.

The common man feels entitled to a level of corruption
    reserved for the elite in the West.
Truckers behave like Wall Street
Try to sell what they don't own.

We stop and show our papers when the police point at our car.
Everyone else pours petrol on the problem.
They can't hide behind Hillary Clinton.

While the rest of the world gets weak when hit or neglected
The opposite happens here—
Defiance through decay—

She holds a sword high above Volgograd for the forgetful.

Temporarily Without Proof

Lost in the land that weaponized attrition
My hands are frantic
Bleeding due to the friction against everything we own
Searching in the dark

I lost it
Patrick's passport
He is a person without proof

I look up to see I'm being watched
By a man in sandals with a holstered handgun
I will sleep in his hotel
Knowing
My carelessness destroyed my dream
In the mirror everything I hate about myself is bigger
        and everything I like is smaller

As soon as the sun hits I start to search
Behind a lip in the glove box
I find Patrick's permission to exist in this time and space

I cannot contain my excitement in front of
The man in sandals with a holstered handgun
His sympathetic smile reveals a tooth as golden as my future

Hearts and Minds

In the sliver of space between giants
guns and documents collaborate
every person in their place, or else
search items to seek intent
a place to roll over and show your belly, promptly
before a monotonous mind knows it loses control of you.

I hand our passports to the Kazakh border guard.
In excitement he yells:

"AMERICA, BARACK OBAMA, WHITNEY HOUSTON"

2 AM Kazakhstan

The last gas station before Kazakhstan had three employees:
cashier, attendant, guard with an AK-47.

We wonder about the purpose of the latter
as exhaustion whittles our options down to sleeping
     next to a broken road
straighten synthetic sticks to construct a barrier of nylon.

All sounds in the night are loaded with crying mothers
infrequent engines push pairs of lights
     past the range of paranoia,
except this pair—this pair wants something.

All levels of undressed and relaxation are rapidly repaired
     in preparation of the approaching lights.

Stand and wait.
Is it the land owners?

        stand and wait

Is it robbers?

             stand and wait

    or worse?

The lights end their approach.
Two men spill out of the van.
There may be more inside.

As they walk with the light to their backs
    the light in our eyes
    the contents of their hands
    hidden as their intent.

                                        stand and wait

We don't share a language to project peace
        across the distance in the dark.

                                        stand and wait

We bet heavily on best intentions.
If anyone chooses violence
the first to choose it usually wins.

Who is willing to do the worst thing first?
        stand and wait

All bellies are soft in a world of propelled and sharpened steel.
But do not create a situation we have to win out of nothing,
        do not be wrong.
Venerability must outlast miscommunication.

Their hands contain beer—
The moment for pure aggression fades into a game of charades
        where the right answer will never be revealed.
Misunderstanding can rebuild all that has faded.

We think they want to if the road gets better.
We think we tell them it doesn't.
We think we ask if we can sleep here.
We think they say no when they point at the distance.

I start to disassemble the tent
        they stop me.
We think they say, look how big this place it is
        of course you can stay here.

Smiles as all of us part.
Nothing lost that cannot be replaced.

We have a lot to learn about a land with no fences.

We wake up in someone's yard sticky from the sun
With a better understanding of
     how wars no one wants
     get started.

Who Did You Meet My Green Eyed Son?

My face projects a pulse, a rhythm
that prompts a ballet of extra effort.
Enhanced smiles, exaggerated greetings, expedited steps.
I am trapped in a quiet understanding
      that my life is worth a little bit more.

Repeated so often it has clotted into truth
      an embolism in the arteries of the world.

If my eyes take the easy way and follow the pretty pirouette
I will never see the world.
I bait the ballerina with my heart and wallet.

Trust a stranger who will be gone tomorrow
      with your cash flow, safety, and social standing.

Ignore this hateful rhythm.
Dance the way you always have.
I want to learn.

I have come a long way to see
Your blood flow without obstruction

But we are waiting for a hard rain.

Driving

We rattle forward in between two piles of upside down dirt
      that make a canyon
carved by a river of pistons that flow from an underground lake
      a new silk road
that will carry too many products to be named
      after any one of them.

Somewhere in this sea of grass
that knows it must stretch toward the sun.

Man first put a leg over the back of a horse
could move faster than he could run
and found a new speed of appetite.

A 1.2 liter Engine

When driving East
you have
to get up
early

because
every few days
you
lose

an
hour of
daylight

until you
find
yourself on
the streetlightless
side of the
world

and
what
everyone you know
thinks is
noon
now
looks like

Midnight

The Formation of Dingus Kahnvoy

at the narrowest point of the funnel
strange Westerners poor themselves into—

after import tax and dumplings   (timing is everything)
we are abruptly welded in permanence to each other
we go without rest

Seven craving new fun
4 American
3 British
3 cars

in a place where eagles in bondage travel by motorcycle
preprogrammed series of actions are unknowable
possibility returns to logarithmic
we bebop in and out of boyhood in the blundering bodies of men
savoring the wild grasp dance of the return to turbo curiosity

we award the dumbest of the day
laughter fills all gaps of competence

freer than roads
we sleep with the wind
one of the great things I will do
I will do with six others

for the brothers of the breakdown it is Ulaanbaatar or bust

Supplement to Navigation

We are not where we think we are.
We have crossed the pink line on paper, but

    we still say thank you in Kazakh: рақмет сізге

Until it is та бүхэнд баярлалаа, we are in a Muslim country

So we ask permission before we crack beers.
It is always granted,

    but it would be impolite
    to navigate by map alone.

The Steppe

The   empire

of

horse

and

wind

spilled

s   o   much blood

that it didn't need   stone to be

remembered

.

i ride horses

and

wrestle with strangers

in

        this

place   that

can make

a pile
of rocks
and plastic bags
holy

like I'm touching a

Roman

short sword
.

Dust

wind

caress

my skin

as

i

drive

for

days

and

days

it

looks

like i

have
not

                                        moved at all.

                                                When

          i   see

the same

endless

of

GRASS.[1]

---

[1] Will I have something beautiful
enough to say about humanity
to justify all the Benzene I burned?

Night Pooping on the Outskirts of the Gobi Desert

Canned ram meat has set a fuse.
I can no longer hide from the high desert cold.

Devoid of distraction
I am a man
squatting over a hole
in an emptiness

required to see the absurdity of infinity
contained in the sky

the crippling beauty of the before during and after
of countless explosions at once.

I am too small not to be enormous.
I have trained my ankles and knees
to function outside of modernity
and have finally found a position capable
of cleaning the core of me
without waste.

I am connected
to something too big
to be practical.

Too Hot to Roll the Windows Down

dust
price of movement
finds all holes
and sinks
clogs
in-between the keys
grits and grind

failure
is in the air

a dirty shirt
migrates to cover
the intake holes
of a red face
sharing the sun
with the memory of
lips on my ribs

failure
is in the air

forward

in East
answers to
a question no one asked

I chase a question to better ask it?

*Later
in the cold night
my ribs rest
on the rocks
goats graze around
the memory of her face

the lips of her lion face
wait for me

next to the failure
in the air.

A Nomad Smile

He does not strain to hold the world he was made for
    he fits and is.

The constant chisel of marketing
    is yet to make him fragile in his home.

Understanding himself in calm totality
    allows him to share without fear.

This hard place will starve the selfish.

The steppe is his birth right.
Free to move to a land time has welded him to
    he follows the grass.
The herd grazes the way it always has:
    under a passed-down guidance.

Most of the songs that land in his ears
    came from the mouths he feeds with his hands.

The life of the family can be no better
    than the aggregate of their ability
    but it can be worse.

An undistracted joy radiates for a body
    brittle and strong
    from a life of hard purpose.

I sip from a slow simmer of life
I thought had died with my grandparents.

Knowing Where to Look

on a seemingly flat stretch of field
a schoolboy challenge asked and answered

a race
to nowhere
ambition disturbs the dirt
as egos push against it for speed
in the thrill of the moment the rest of the moments
are momentarily forgotten
unexpected topography brings them all crashing back
the car drops
the bumper finds the land before the wheels
dirt pushes back against our egos and takes her speed back
the car folds
rubber rubs the frame
after some fiddling and testing
we proclaim the death of a Suzuki Alto

Patrick and Sam go for help
we find ourselves treading water in our own testosterone spill,
throwing rocks that land and disturb the dirt

Patrick and Sam return with a truck and two drivers
back up to a hill and push the car in the bed and strap it down

I sit on Sam's lap as we bump and rattle
back to the driver's house
step over a baby bathing in a bucket
sit down and drink horse milk
everyone finishes before me and
the driver's breast feeding wife
and leaves

my instinct is to look away
she must want privacy

I am being rude
in her home
I'm the one breaking cars
she is building

I look up at the source of everything I have come to see
the trickle that brings life to the dirt I disturb
where the rubber meets the road
mother flows into child

Arrival

everything has permission to collapse as a success
in the parking lot behind the hotel
a density of people
nature and breakdown are no longer
the hindrance to movement

with dogs tied to them
discarded cars will become cash for an orphanage
the former containers of candy from the West collected into piles

depression of success will have to wait
first its components will have to be dismantled
titles will have to go to the right people

interceptors always flock to exchanges
watch and compete with quick cash for the newly useless
we sell only what never contained a purpose for us
and keep an eye on everything else
good intentions need an escort

the worst part of traveling has always been arriving
tomorrow there is nowhere to go but drunk

Test of Skill

An open challenge on the wall of the hostel:

Can you walk the streets of U.B. for an hour
     with a backpack on
and return with the zipper closed?

MONGOLIAN STRIP CLUB

It is sexy sax night at the Marco Polo Club. Through the closed pizza restaurant and up the stairs. The younger members of Dingus Kahnvoy don't want to pay the cover. You have to be the change you want to see in the world, I think as I pay the man.

Wrapped in neon fabrics, the women of the Montana of Asia gently sway with a beauty that demands to be pregnant. Western men whose bodies have been eroded by ergonomic chairs and plopped into khakis awkwardly jab at rhythm as they try to alter the proximity of their wiggling.

> There is no stage.
> No separation.
> Poles haphazardly connect the floor to the ceiling.

A man in a white tuxedo plays a saxophone over a recorded track of The Lady in Red. Mediocre scotch recklessly priced. My restraint hates her Dad and just hops on Evel Knievel's motorcycle. As I walk from one scotch to the next, I prance with one of the ladies. As an American in the former Eastern Bloc, my dancing abilities are overestimated due to the proximity of my everyday life to black people.

The announcer calls for my attention to the two fully clothed gymnasts. I better slow down, drink a beer.

A mouth guard is elevated on a metal pole a foot-and-a-half from the ground. The gymnast laying on her stomach bites it, pushes against the floor. Turns herself into the letter C, with her ass above her head, belly button in the air. Fully supported by her teeth. A hula hoop is put on each leg and rotated. Yelling is the only response. If only I had the ability to buy her a Dodge Caravan.

They disappear as quickly as I fell in love.
She punched me in the physics.

4000tögrög
more scotch

8 women dressed up as princess Jasmine appear, do nothing, then leave. And then it is heard: "AND NOW MAKE SOME NOISE FOR DROP KNIVES ON HIM." A shirtless man in hammer pants has brought knives. He hands them to an assistant and lays down. The knives are held high in the air, then dropped onto his stomach. They bounce. Tonight there will be no penetration. One bed of nails is placed on the floor and another on his stomach. A man who intends to send mineral wealth far away from here is selected from the crowd to stand on the nails and man sandwich. The sandwich stays solid under the weight of the future. When did women who don't work here get here?

I yell and drink as I contemplate a life well lived. Across the room the will and goals of 15 men suddenly become divisible by two. Depressed nervous systems command blubber to collide and compete to be beach master. After all this time we still hear the music that makes an amoeba mean, all the time. Patrick double-checks that my pacifism is still intact. Of course I want to see how this goes from here. The bouncer's arrival melts the dream of alpha. Will and goals evaporate. Without a dream, 15 individuals stand confused. Now that they are too smart to fight, they comply with his order to exit.

"AND NOW SOMETHING FOR THE LADIES," calls the announcer.

Two men arrive, one with a leather mask over his face. Their abs are spectacular. Within a minute-and-a-half, both of their outfits are thrust into the air. Leather thongs will no longer wait behind pants. The floor is vigorously humped. I don't think they have figured out the business model for taking men's money to look at naked women. I hope they never do. Me and Patrick are so happy. The rest of the Western men are uncomfortable aboard this freight train of male sexuality. Their muscular buttocks don't stop ramming their bulges into the ground, exposing their string-covered taints and buttholes. I drink in support. I vote for this. I don't remember if I chanted "USA," but according to my values I probably did.

"AND NOW SOMETHING ELSE FOR THE LADIES!"

They need three male volunteers. Sam is up for it. He loves Crunch and Munch, and is unfazed by mayhem. Dingus Kanhvoy is represented, as well as the Western baby boomers and a local man. These fine stallions will compete for the shouting of the ladies. The Mongolian is pretty, the baby boomer is rich, but they are not men of chaos. As in all sexual acts, enthusiasm is important. Sam's pants hit the ceiling fan as well as his foot. His shoe flies off as he inverts himself on a pole in his boxer shorts. The bouncer, fearing property damage and injury, must corral Sam's free-form improvisational sexual expression. After the fury the fellow slut gladiator from Mongolia pulls Sam's boxer shorts away to look at his penis. He wants to see if the stereotype is true. No one could blame him. Sam wins a 30-day free entry coupon. Since I am also staying longer, he tries to convince them to make it a 15-day pass for two people. When they ask him his name, he tells them it is Matt and Sam. I drink enough scotch for them to agree. We are instructed not to shave or they will not recognize us. We all look the same.

The strippers are back, tits out. A parade of lap dances begins. If you lean forward it means you want to be left alone; if you lean back, you will be straddled and charged about three bucks. Civilization is worth it. I feel like I haven't been bathing weekly and eating canned ram. The formerly competing blobs of men are let back into the lap dance bonanza. The women thank us and leave. I feel as if I could not buy any of them. I like that. I may be wrong, but it feels like they own their bodies. They have roles, but fear doesn't keep them there. Once again, I could be wrong. The oppressor always wants to believe he is gaining because of the consent of the oppressed.

More drinking. We meet a man who works for Bloomberg out here. That is our asshole mayor. Some Australian dickbag says our new friend looks and sounds Chinese. The rage of a baby duck is mustered into the worst slap ever. The bouncer asks us what happened. I say, "That asshole said that guy looks Chinese." The Aussie is asked to leave. Patrick and I reassure him that he does not look Chinese. I ask the bouncer for a job. He says I should try the other strip club in town and writes down their number. They need big guys who speak English. I have second thoughts in the morning, and no longer consider looking Chinese an insult.

You Can Always Depend on the Kindness of Strangers

In the aftermath of a street fight
I run down the stairs with Patrick
to the unconscious man we were watching from the balcony.

As I feel the breath of his open airway push against my hand

we are approached by one of the fighters who ran a way:

"Please leave I beg of you"

he says with a panicked sinkhole of complexity in his eyes.

The Smile that Turned North to South

tiny butterfly engine
in the space she takes
soft wings and steel

taught herself English by watching movies
shows me the work her ad agency does in Bucharest

she hitchhiked to Mongolia
to see a shaman
a carrier of questions

I want to put my hand on her stomach
feel the pulse of her curiosity
feel it flash on the other side of her skin

Before we leave she says, "one rule:

no love
don't dream about me "

I arrange the rusty gates inside myself
around what I need to keep clear
give her a corral to stomp in

for a burst
I'm going to be her horse

Let Go

two bodies in discommunication

no harmony of attack and retreat

until

on my back

I lose my projections
I listen and hear enough to know I need more

Negotiating a Guide

I would have agreed on a little lower than the first price
but I am an American puppy too in love with the world.
Nervous, not wanting to offend.

She is a business woman
the engine of her idea
who chased butterflies in the time of CEAUCESCU.

Just be huge
and let her do the talking
for cash savings.

Get em' babe:
Dynamic women give me a boner.

A Lovely Day in Tsagaasaanur in Three Parts

Part One

Unwrap the noodle brick and boil over propane.
Her tongue keeps another lover to see if I break.
I set off to find my own fun, before
Possibility is herniated under the weight of safety.

I wander amongst the horses and dogs
    in-between the hills.
A stranger waves me over. I begin to help.
They are building a temporary house older than my civilization.
I have the hands of a 15-year-old touching a breast.
Every movement without the luxury of repetition and time,
    to sever the tangents of disaster.

I am useless.
They move with the confidence of a single outcome,
    and have no time for my detours, but

My new friend's toddler daughter and I share
    a curiosity for our new surroundings.
I chase her in and out of possibilities.
She tries to scrape and pull the hair from my face and arms.
It stands in defiance of how all other people look,
    so she pets me. I take a place
    between a man and a dog.
She teaches me words.
We bounce in the world that will build her.

From elements to the headquarters of an empire in hours.
If I follow fingers I am a qualified forklift
    for blankets and cell phone chargers.
Finished, we drink milk from an unbroken history of horses.

For a piece of time I am a part of this.

Part Two

Unwrap the noodle brick and boil over propane. The safety of the morning is falling with the sun. I'm going to find more of her. *But chaos is now!* Metal has fallen, people are screaming, I run and remember my E.M.T. class, hoping not to see my first unprepared corpse. Seven half-drunk men are still fully attached to themselves, but they have spilled the van that brought me here. The rear axle is sticking out of the wheel well. We stare at a pile incapable of its purpose. The pointed end of a 15-foot former tree is jammed in between the bumper and the ground. We fulcrum just enough to fit a jack three feet too short underneath. A wood block is found from the yard, and put under a second, equally-underqualified jack. I'm appointed to be tall and stabilize one side of the van. As alternating Jenga towers grow block by block, a chainsaw is brought out when the yard runs out of scraps. Every new block brings two pillars closer to the brink of being projectiles. The proper height is reached as the sun leaves the day. A man climbs underneath. Drunk, determined in the dark, an above-ground miner is digging. Paint chips crack and press into my soft palms under the pressure of a slight sway. They rattle from the vibration of a hammer colliding to make space for an obstinate axle. Eyes and fingers communicate what ears and mouths cannot. If the unknown physics of rusty metal is stickier than the improvised association of wooden blocks, this man will die. Unavailability and courage will kill him, or maybe me not understanding the language in which vital commands are shouted. The wood is sticky enough. His triumph will take me home in a few days. They pass vodka and I am allowed a swig.

For a piece of time I am a part of this.

Part Three

A fire radiates inside iron, reflects off of tin
    and back into our room
    to boil away the poison of our pasts.
Our love has this time and place.
When either run out, she trusts I will kill it.
I trust her to keep me from contaminating
    the parts of her she needs.

My hands no longer belong to a fifteen-year-old.
They seek and take, stalk and set traps.

We pull pieces of rage out of each other.
I watch the power of my temporary tiger.
The heat in her skin drips a trail
To what she wants to watch me destroy.

We find revenge in each other
Dislodge what has been choking the other.
An open airway for a few easy breaths in a lovely world.

For a piece of time I don't have to part from her.

The Death of Wilderness

In a town too remote to sell condoms
they are still celebrating Lebron James' victory in the finals.
My new friend learned English from Marv Albert,
        he tells me, loudly.

Our horse guide to the shaman people
spent half the ride on a cell phone.

In the place I chose to test myself against the elements
where I had planned to write my chapter of man vs. nature
every six hours friendly herders gave me dried cheese.

Where I planned to help, equipped with just where I was born,
the man who helped me buy pants to keep me from
        succumbing to the elements
works in publishing—he downloaded a
        Mongolian-to-English dictionary
        on the hotel WiFi, to tell me this.

I am now aware of how little I have to offer.

I procured fresh drinking water
by first visiting the ATM.
The unused water purification kit
I had no intention of using in Europe
will only remove the sediment in me.

Land misunderstood by me, never unused.
Always in someone's

                grocery store,
                daily commute
                or playground.

The expansionist delusions of my gunfighter nation

have bored into the space where my dreams are born.
As I scrape the racism from my reptile
I see the faces of individuals.

At a teepee with a satellite dish on a stick
      by the Russian border
I have chased a myth to attrition
A justification of conquerors has starved in my mind.

The world is not my ego treadmill.
People live here.

Shaman Vomit

I will vomit once in Eurasia, despite
the frequency with which
the dart of my finger is flung at Cyrillic menus.

The afterlife is different in this tepee:
It has the power to touch and take from some.
Children will dig their own graves in their sleep.
Without guidance they will crawl in.

The moon was wrong
but she saw a need in us.

She put on a suit of bones
for the sprits to fill so they can meet
close enough to convey the message.
Far from the madness is still too close to the madness.
Vodka, cigarettes and a 20,000 note is fair
        to put her through this.
She drums, dances, and chants past when the fire freezes out.
I have my answer: My family will farm again.

It is a cold night to sleep with my head next to a spiritbag
I need to find a flashlight before this flies out of me.
In front of the moon and the reindeer I serve an eviction.
As my rejection finds soil I am surrounded by dogs
Growling, barking, biting to compete to eat what I have left.
I cannot get bit—I am 2 days from a hospital.

In the morning I try to find and clean the vomit
        but there is nothing left.
Our guide tells the Shaman about my problems last night.
I'm told to get rid of a pair of boots back home
        that are holding me back.

Brown Ropers, work boot of the cowboy.

I took them from the barn to the bar.
They used to protect my feet from the goo of celebration
        and the foot stomps of the belligerent.
I wore them while putting every biker, banker, and bro
        in a headlock.
The dogs have a better use for all of that now.

Bad Sex on a Stomach Bug

I have shit out all my power, but I still have to have her

    tan

        lean

            last chance

the way back to the peace I never had

    in the other bed

the fleeting answer to the problem of always

but what I have to offer in exchange for real butter
    does not work
    deprived and dying just enough to disappoint
this night will have no lights

I lick up every drop of redemption my tongue
    can get its fingers on
chasing the forgiveness in her explosion

    tan

        lean

            last chance

before I lose her

The End of a Tender Tap

I taste the salt of ourselves on her lips
        This bottom bunk will be our last
    We cannot cling tighter than time

                                The crowbar always wins.

"If you are in Europe, find me and fuck me"......!!!!........?....?

                                          "I will!"

"If you are in America, find me and fuck me" ......?.....?........!!!!!

                                        "I will!"

                        "I want what you want for you"
"I want what you want for you"

                   "good bye"

"good bye"

                            The door always the door.

gone

Korea

The wind is done being wild and whispers *Itaewon*.
My ascent of Hooker Hill elicits sudden hellos
From behind ever door, window, and stone.
Did I walk through a forest of tally marks
      on the human trafficking index?
Feeding on the compost of the U.S defense budget?
Perhaps, says the price of my bed

A room of my own.
I can sit when I shit but I have traded the stars.
Amongst the Dashikis and bulgogi
I find some Marines who get me drunk enough
      to forget I speak English.
Niet—I cross my arms—*Niet Niet.*
They have a curfew in this neighborhood
Due to the rapes of their comrades.
Grandmas on the street feed us meat sticks and pig faces.

Soul music calls me into a coffee shop.
Egg and Pixie dress in Technicolor.
Mesmerized by their space beauty
I stare into my memories, confused

by the kind of GDP that makes poop solid
that stacks people doing paper work high enough
      to scratch the clouds.

I glide on a bus to the ocean.
Somewhere beyond the powers of my eyes ingestion
East becomes West and I have a wedding to attend.

A proper wild man knows when it is time for a Diflucan.

San Francisco Layover

I am the coat they drape over James Brown.
Stamp me a citizen, Ma'am.

                    The overweight are confused
                        by clear, well-lit signage.
        Narrow skill creates an indefensible wealth.
            I want to rob them on principle,
                    and pay my guide more.

                    Everything at once always.
        A Power Bar rests in a fanny pack,
                            just in case.

                    San Francisco to Seattle:
            7 days distance in a few hours
        miles of beauty and frustration wasted.
                    Punctuality is key.
        When consuming from tube to tube,
            the place most in need of screams
            has the least tolerance for them.

How does such a magnificent chair repetitively exist?
        For the ass of anyone, let alone the ass of all?
Drive-Through breastfeed me, America.
I'll complain when my mouth has time,
In between fire hosings of wasteful kindness,
I won't fight you.

Thank You.

Handicap Access, National Parks, and the Highway System
The Three Great Beacons of the American Attempt

Those with a common origin can celebrate walls that separate
    that kept them safe from the other.
We are an aggregate of the other
    consistently failing at the ideas
    that bind us to each other.

Brilliance has no pattern of distribution.
Ideas die quickly without a witness, decay into a disequilibrium
    for a precarious people.
Ramps, buttons, rails, bathrooms and parking spaces.
We will reverse engineer form limitation to expression
    in all schools.
We will defy our plagues in public spaces.
The tragedies that take our sacred movement
    will be no indication of worth.
We build for all because we believe in all
In bright contradiction to our failures.

Pick your god or don't.
All can dance in the crushing silence, howling roar,
    or tickling whisper of creation.
We will protect a beauty too grandiose to be captured
    and transported by art.
Trade the niceties of ambition for the honesty of indifference.
There is no substitute for the power contained in these lands
    that turn time into a ruler
    to measure our progress against the debts of existence.
Wheel your grandma to hear the same siren call
    that will compel active others to flirt with their demise.
We will protect it from monopoly and destruction.
We preserve for all because we believe in all
In bright contradiction to our failures.

From the children of wars to the parents who fought in them

to the families who are strangers to rage
lies an asphalt to challenge Icarus,
smooth without end across a continent.
At all hours every byproduct of the endeavor of man and woman
will cause vulcanized rubber to spin.
We cling to each other across the space that defines us.
By ease of moment on ribbons of restlessness
we collide cultures into our own
dependent on proximity to disagreement to take us closer
to a dream that has never been done.
We connect to all because we believe in all
In bright contradiction to our failures.

We have built these three great beacons out of necessity
To keep the dark created by walls from coagulating
into our collapse
In bright contradiction to the great crimes that keep the lights on
in this idea, this attempt.
In bright contradiction to our failures,
We are access to each other.

The Dream of Dakota

America is so big it can contain its own diaspora.
I will return to the land of my grandparents.
Deep underneath what the wind left of the upside-down sod
They found the heroin of movement.
I will help with a harvest.

In the harsh land that taught my grandma to make stew,
      taught my grandfather to work,
Less than a hundred miles from a foreclosed farm
      that taught generations to fear debt.

I want to feel my hands freeze
Chasing the undistracted joy of a hard purpose
An attempt to be wedged into a place by time
As I work to pay for a comfortable landing in Brooklyn.

When the car part arrives
I will depart with Mr. and Mrs. Pooper for the Bakken.

Heritage Marker

The dead must be tired of hearing
how hard it was for their killers to get here,

      and how far they traveled

            to kill them,

and how much furniture they had to leave on the prairie

                  to take everything.

A Familiar Face

My name is Camaro Pregnant
I get hot babes pregnant in New Mexico
in the back of an El Camino
I chose the name Camaro for the musicality

I keep the callouses of empire on my palms
I was in 'Nam when you were in Mom
betrayed by spotted owls and Jane Fonda
I have no time for caution

The Secretariat of the proletariat
I am strong and fast
if I break my leg
they will shoot me

A gas station gourmet
I make my Rice Crispy Treats with Fruity Pebbles
delicately inserting synthetic cheese into hotdogs
all rivers, roofs, and fields are my Riviera

I wash my woman's hair with beer that I leave in the sun
the heat and bubbles tingle her scalp
I teach my children how to make a manufactured home or trailer
        a spa
so they never learn how to make a prison ass with a latex glove

I am a goddam water slide renegade
full of discount fire works
I live in the moment
but I am the opposite of Buddhism

It ain't easy being greazy, kid

Boom, Bust and Goodbye

There are too many Boy Scouts
who believe the knots they learned to tie
had something to do with freedom.

Rubbing their broken lives together
the women born here avoid the new men.

We drink in the afternoon
in the yard of what was a highway rest stop turned into a house
        with one bedroom   two baths.
Bring the flatscreen outside
enjoy the weather while it lasts
fire a few shells into the air.

There are too many extended cabs to cross
        to make a left turn
        into America's most profitable Taco Bell.
Good wages, no life.
Just testosterone and flaming holes in the ground.

No work, the company folded.
Just the All You Can Eat Pizza Ranch
the trailer that no one weatherized.
No heat; the toilet water is ice.
Sacrifice one of my sleeping space heaters.
I see my breath as I eat my hand-me-down Fruit Loops.
Watch the clock until it's time to go to
the new multimillion-dollar community center.

The company hired me because I have a driver's license.
That puts me ahead of most the employees
who used to have something to do
        and needed someone to drive them there.
We're supposed to roll out mats that keep oil spills
        from contaminating.

Land tampons.
No regulation demands it, so no one buys it.
Protection means a future.

No calls coming in.
An offer to drive all night to Tacoma
is too tempting to turn down.
Thanksgiving at home
Then back to New York.
If I have to pay NY prices I want to walk downstairs
        and hear about what books the
New York women are reading.

When the Trickle Down Lands

1:01 AM an empty bar car plows through the Dakota dark
a small man
traveling partner of Bucket Man
sleeps in a seat

    "Bucket Man Rolling Down the Streets of Everywhere"[2]

and I discuss the utility of a 5 gallon bucket

he sits on it and begs on a street corner in America
sympathy goes stale in 3 days and he rolls his bucket
to another street corner in America

his heart won't work well enough for him to work
berate him all you want it still won't

when held in belittled hands
bootstraps behave like a whip

an able-bodied oil man
10 beers, a few kids and a mortgage deep
overhears and wants to regrow the size he sacrifices
      to borrow his pot to piss in
he hears the drum thump that makes an amoeba mean
find fault, to damn fragility
pretend morality will keep him off a bucket

"I never took a handout in my life."

                          "Good for you."

"I worked for everything I ever got."

                          "I wish I could."

---

[2] Sung to the tune of Elton John's "Rocket Man"

"You need to get off your ass and quit living off of ME."

"I never asked you for anything."

"You can work, you just don't want to."

The flood of being fragile leaks
clings to his nose a Spartan against accumulated gravity, then
falls to the floor flying on rails to the next street corner
        in America
1:25 AM in an empty bar car plowing through the Dakota dark
there is only one seat that will soothe the cascade of Bucket Man

                "Wake Up."

                "Move."

a small man looks for somewhere else to be

Being Driven

Electricity runs to the millions of manmade pinpricks in the
darkness

>   I ride across a river that used to be an obstacle
>   To find a flash amongst the stacks of worlds.

Under the right alchemy the evening can turn into a run-on
sentence.

This ease feels an impossible dream
In contrast to the memories of dust
That always seemed to settle where it started.

She is Happy

The price is paid upon return

In the eyes that will never see me with the same lust again

I chose to leave this warmth

For an unknown collection of

                                  cold and boiling beautiful memories

                    We sit and I tell her about a few of them

As a present tense memory.

Return to Ritual

they came to the bar
ordered a product
I brought it
collected money

my bad attitude stopped the room

I offered no part of myself
only what was paid for

"excuse me"

I just got back from a place where consumption wasn't scarred

"Thanks for coming out tonight,
it is so good to see you,
have a great evening."

Return to Ritual 2

A fence means ownership is more important than movement.
For years my profession has been
Wrestling a musicality
That measures itself by
What it can displace
What it can consume
What it can dominate
What it can destroy
by the size of the stains it can create
into a place where it is still safe to sell it alcohol
then praise it for the transaction
Like a horse kicking a stall
I'm running out of patience for my box.

A Nice Lie, If Only for an Evening

Feeling stretched and threadbare because
     I don't contain enough cloth
       to drag across and absorb the world.
Lifting armoires, cleaning glasses, waking dogs
       and stopping fights
       trying to collect
       enough cash to find a bed
To dream about more maps from

I wore the pair of pants with the smaller hole in them on a date.
She had a softness that might have radiated
       with the ability to stop.
In her I projected a salvation from sleeping on couches.
Sparks from fireworks are safe because
       there is nothing for them to catch
       that high in the air.

We sit at the same table, but
We leave on different sidewalks.

She is in love with someone else.
I will be in love with somewhere else.

The Night I Became a Memory of Myself

Mothers spend hours and hours and hours of milk
Pull patience out of parts of themselves they didn't have before
        they were mothers
Step on scattered blocks on the floor
Absorb the pain   turn it into the framework
        that we hang the future on

So babies can learn to grasp
Learn to stack what they see when they close
        they close their eyes

The hand is the agent of the imagination, fulcrum of creation
Turns matter into a language we can manipulate
Twists the light in ourselves into light others can see

But a fist closes like a door

The intricate bouquet of nerves, bone, meat and tendons
The symphony of milk and time that allows us
        to write symphonies

shuts down

becomes as uncomplicated and cold as a hammer without nails
        to build with beautiful patient intricacy

        becomes a fast moving thud

As fists ricochet off the container I keep myself in. The container
that grew from a

        baby learning to stack blocks

I lick my teeth
To see if they have broken

Brain Injury

When consciousness is gone it is gone
You only see it as it comes
back to you

Death. Of self in liv   es in the broken container of self.

reality through the br n0oken screen   broken self.

In my sleep a demon baby tries to eat my penis
I wake to sleep punch   ing my self in the crotch.

In a shower the falling water I have a fraction of is the only
ancho to a previous conciouness I am broken. That is all.iam
until..?FUUUUKKKCCCC do not commit suicde un(til you have
exhaust)ted that this is the only way out. You owe it to those
who love and feed d you.
Vibrae in yoiur brokenness until you

                                   drip back into yourself.

My mother loves me. I will owe my return to her :after I sleep.
IM so sorry sorry sorry sorry sorry sorry sory ssory ssoorry
sorry sorry soory ssoryy sorry sorry sooyr ssoyy sorry soory
sorry FUCK sorry sorry ssory ssory ssooy ssorry ssiojnsory
ssory ssosfuy sorry sorry . sorry sososoy souyrd7 iodklczm ,m.
jdcry sur cry sory cory dsory sor y yyydkdcicj soryyry caAfn
good bye to what once was. Sorry

I can no lo nger   s ta n d.

I can't ev ery thi ng

because I caannnot wake up.
 I WAKE UP IN FEAR!
I wwakeu pinfea.r sorr y

About the Author

Matthew Eiford-Schroeder was raised in Camas, Washington, where he spent a sizable portion of his time working and playing on his grandparents' cattle farm. He moved around America by working retail and lifting heavy things. Eventually he landed in New York, where he snuck into an art school and became a bouncer. He currently lives in Bellingham, WA, where he is studying political science at Western Washington University.

PRINTED MATTER VANCOUVER
we write because we must

Printed Matter Vancouver is a small press that provides editing, writing coaching, and book development services. We work with new, emerging, and established writers of poetry, memoir, and fiction, although we also have a unique set of skills in journalism, technical writing, and academic essays.

Our main purpose is to assist writers in developing their skills by providing support, constructive feedback, and useful guidance. Are you a part-time writer, a poet, a creative fiction writer, someone who wants to write a memoir for family members, or are you looking to work with an editor on your existing manuscript? Some of our clients are focused on getting their work out into the world through the submission process. Whatever path you see yourself on, our unique coaching process will help you get the job done.

We begin with the writer's goals and as a team focus on a plan with a set of steps. Our services include editing, coaching, workshops, manuscript layout/design, format, and production. We can provide you with the tools to self-publish, or to get your work ready to submit for publication. All initial consultations are for sixty minutes and are free of charge.

As a small press, we do not accept unsolicited manuscripts for publication by Printed Matter Vancouver. Please feel free to contact us with any questions you may have about our services.

Toni Lumbrazo Luna, Editor, Publisher
Christopher J. Luna, Editor, Publisher, and
Past Clark County Poet Laureate (2013-2017)

www.printedmattervancouver.com
printedmattervancouver@gmail.com

22785597R00057

Made in the USA
Columbia, SC
02 August 2018